Promise Me the Stars

Also by Poppy Fraser

Fantastic Recipes from my Favourite People

10 Minute Suppers for Children

Promise me the Stars

Poems for children
chosen by
Poppy Fraser

First published in Great Britain in 2019 by Fraser Publishing

Copyright in the preface, setting and selection
© Poppy Fraser 2019

Poppy Fraser has asserted her right under the Copyright, Designs and Patents Act 1988 to be identified as the author of this work.

All rights reserved. No part of this publication may be reproduced, stored in a retrieval system or transmitted, in any form or by any means, without the publisher's prior permission in writing.

This book is sold subject to the condition that it shall not, by way of trade or otherwise, be lent, resold, hired out or otherwise circulated without the publisher's prior consent in any form of binding or cover other than that in which it is published and without a similar condition, including this condition, being imposed on the subsequent purchaser.

Extract from 'When We Were Very Young' by A. A. Milne. Text copyright © The Trustees of the Pooh Properties 1924. Published by Egmont UK Ltd and used with permission.

Every reasonable effort has been made to trace copyright holders of material reproduced in this book, but if any have been inadvertently overlooked the publishers would be glad to hear from them.

Edited, designed and produced by Tandem Publishing Limited: http://tandempublishing.yolasite.com/

ISBN: 978-1-5272-4456-6
10 9 8 7 6 5 4 3 2 1

A CIP catalogue record for this book is available from the British Library.

Printed and bound in Great Britain by CPI Group (UK) Ltd, Croydon CR0 4YY

For my own children, Lorcan, Bertie, Pom and Jacobi…

… and in memory of the beloved children my friends have lost.

Contents

Preface   xi

The Animal Kingdom   1

Magpies in Picardy by T. P. Cameron Wilson • The Lamb by William Blake • The Tyger by William Blake • *From* A Song to David by Christopher Smart • The Mountain and the Squirrel by Ralph Waldo Emerson • Something Told the Wild Geese by Rachel Field • The Frog by Hilaire Belloc • The Owl and the Pussy-Cat by Edward Lear • The Donkey by G. K. Chesterton • Four Feet by Rudyard Kipling • Jim by Hilaire Belloc • Jabberwocky by Lewis Carroll • Everyone Sang by Siegfried Sassoon

Love   19

The Bargain by Sir Philip Sidney • Annabel Lee by Edgar Allan Poe • Bessie's Song to her Doll by Lewis Carroll • Carpe Diem by Laurence Hope • Eros by Ralph Waldo Emerson • I am only the house of your beloved by Rumi • Bonnie Charlie by Lady Nairne • Aedh Wishes for the Cloths of Heaven by William Butler Yeats • Remember by Christina Rossetti • Y'sod adapted from Ba'al Shem Tov • The Gift of Love by Robert Burns • *From* the *Divine Comedy* by Dante • Love by R. G. Ingersoll • 'When two souls…' by Victor Hugo • *Paradiso* XVIII by Dante

Courage & Strength 37

Invictus by W. E. Henley • I Vow to Thee, My Country by Cecil Spring-Rice • Border Ballad by Sir Walter Scott • The Soldier by Rupert Brooke • Jerusalem by William Blake • The Lord is My Shepherd, Psalm 23

Dreamland 45

Dreamland by Lewis Carroll • *From* Goblin Market by Christina Rossetti • Ozymandias by Percy Bysshe Shelley • Christ in the Stranger's Guise • Walk a Little Slower, Daddy • The Courtship of the Yonghy-Bonghy-Bò by Edward Lear • When I Consider How My Light is Spent by John Milton • Up-Hill by Christina Rossetti • The Naughty Brother by Bertie Hughes • Brother and Sister by Lewis Carroll • A Fairy Went A-Marketing by Rose Fyleman • Disobedience by A. A. Milne

The Natural World 67

A Charm by Rudyard Kipling • The Fairies by William Allingham • Snowdrops by Mary Vivian • *From* Sir Galahad by Alfred, Lord Tennyson • The Stolen Child by William Butler Yeats • Windy Nights by Robert Louis Stevenson • I Thank Thee, God, That I Have Lived by Elizabeth Craven • Past, Present, Future by Emily Brontë • The Song of the River by William Randolph Hearst • *From Paradise Lost* by John Milton • Why God Made Little Boys

Guidance 85

If by Rudyard Kipling • Sonnet 94 by William Shakespeare • Wisdom by Laurence Hope • The New Colossus by Emma Lazarus • Man's Testament by Adam Lindsay Gordon • Happy The Man by John Dryden • The Cry-Baby by Heinrich Hoffmann • Ithaka by C. P. Cavafy

Historical 97

John of Gaunt's dying speech *from Richard II* • Queen Elizabeth I's Speech at Tilbury • Queen Elizabeth I's Golden Speech

Prayers 103

Gaelic Blessing • Serenity Prayer by Reinhold Niebahr • Gentle Jesus. Meek and Mild by Charles Wesley • Matthew, Mark, Luke and John • Saint Francis of Assisi • A Child's Prayer on Waking • Blessing for a Home, a traditional Jewish blessing • The Supplication of Light, an Islamic prayer • A Child's Bedtime Prayer • 'Where I sit is holy…' • Beloved Lord by Hazrat Inayat Khan • 'As We Are Together…' Thich Nhat Hanh • 'I see the moon…' • Irish Blessing • 'In life…' • 'Our deepest fear…' by Marianne Williamson • Recipe for a Happy Child by Marina Cowdray • 'Courage' by President Kennedy

Acknowledgements 125
Index of Poets 127

Preface

My last two books have been cookbooks, the first put together by asking friends for favourite recipes, the second a mixture of my own recipes and those again given by friends. I enjoyed the collaborative aspect of these, and have known for a long time that I would like to put together another book with the help of friends.

It took a few years to work out exactly what it would be, as I knew I didn't want to write another cookbook. The inspiration came unexpectedly one night – a poetry book for children. I wanted to create something for all ages, a collection to give just as much pleasure to the parent reading as to the small child tucked up in bed, but also including poems for more grown-up children about to fledge the nest. So a broad scope, and full of inspiring and uplifting poems to stir children's minds.

When the thought first came late one night, I began texting friends asking them to tell me their favourite poem. Within a week I had gathered a vast collection of wonderful work. The seed was planted and growing beautifully, the way exciting projects often begin. And it didn't stop with poems: in came quotes and prayers from different religions, and historical speeches sent in by a friend's mother. All of which I believe are important and special, and need to be read by children. The speeches of Elizabeth I are some of the most moving I have ever read, and show such strength and honour and love for her country. Rousing words full of passion – of historical interest, certainly, but also telling of the qualities she possessed as a leader, and inspiring for children.

So although this book is certainly not a cookbook, it is, I believe, a book about something just as important as the food we feed our children: what we feed their minds and consciousness. My hope is that this collection will instil a deep love of words and a respect for the power of poetry to work magic on the soul. So powerful is poetry, it can transport us right into the depths of our beings. As Lord Wavell said, 'Music, mystery and magic are the essence of the highest poetry.' That essence is alive in each and every one of us, and that's what I want children to realise as they read or hear the poems in this little book.

You might think that some of these poems are rather more suited to grown-ups, but I believe in exposing children to art in all its forms as much as possible, and not limiting them. They take what they can, and that is perfect.

The first poem I remember reading was one I was asked to learn and recite at primary school, 'Something Told the Wild Geese' by Rachel Field. It stayed with me, the images and words, and so began a great love of poems. I turn to them when I am searching for somewhere to go and they delicately give something back that is hard to find elsewhere.

My favourite poem in this book is 'Annabel Lee', by Edgar Allen Poe. Unfailingly, it touches the deepest part of me each time I read it. It was published after his death, and explores the themes of the love and death of his beautiful beloved.

I hope this book will give joy to the children who read it, and to the parents who read the poems to their children. I feel so lucky to have worked on this book: everything within is something that I love – for lots of different reasons – and I hope you will share that love too.

—Poppy

***

An important part of the book is that I want to support a new local charity, Treatment Bag, which seeks to offer cancer-treatment patients a little joy at an otherwise extremely difficult time. Treatment Bag provides useful gifts, donated by companies who make things that help those undergoing chemotherapy, like soothing creams and delicious food vouchers. Treatment Bag aims to secure distribution through the NHS and is endorsed by Maggie's Centres. Treatment Bag is entirely funded by donations, and a percentage of the profit of each book will go straight to them.

www.treatmentbag.co.uk

The Animal Kingdom

Magpies in Picardy
T. P. Cameron Wilson

The magpies in Picardy
Are more than I can tell.
They flicker down the dusty roads
And cast a magic spell
On the men who march through Picardy,
Through Picardy to hell.

(The blackbird flies with panic,
The swallow goes with light,
The finches move like ladies,
The owl floats by at night;
But the great and flashing magpie
He flies as artists might.)

A magpie in Picardy
Told me secret things—
Of the music in white feathers,
And the sunlight that sings
And dances in deep shadows—
He told me with his wings.

(The hawk is cruel and rigid,
He watches from a height;
The rook is slow and sombre,
The robin loves to fight;
But the great and flashing magpie
He flies as lovers might.)

He told me that in Picardy,
An age ago or more,
While all his fathers still were eggs,
These dusty highways bore
Brown, singing soldiers marching out
Through Picardy to war.

He said that still through chaos
Works on the ancient plan,
And two things have altered not
Since first the world began—
The beauty of the wild green earth
And the bravery of man.

(For the sparrow flies unthinking
And quarrels in his flight;
The heron trails his legs behind,
The lark goes out of sight;
But the great and flashing magpie
He flies as poets might.)

The Lamb
William Blake

Little Lamb who made thee
    Dost thou know who made thee
Gave thee life and bid thee feed.
By the stream and o'er the mead;
Gave thee clothing of delight,
Softest clothing wooly bright;
Gave thee such a tender voice,
Making all the vales rejoice!
    Little Lamb who made thee
    Dost thou know who made thee

    Little Lamb I'll tell thee,
    Little Lamb I'll tell thee!
He is called by thy name,
For he calls himself a Lamb:
He is meek and he is mild,
He became a little child:
I a child and thou a lamb,
We are called by his name.
    Little Lamb God bless thee.
    Little Lamb God bless thee.

The Tyger
William Blake

Tyger Tyger, burning bright,
In the forests of the night;
What immortal hand or eye,
Could frame thy fearful symmetry?

In what distant deeps or skies.
Burnt the fire of thine eyes?
On what wings dare he aspire?
What the hand, dare seize the fire?

And what shoulder, and what art,
Could twist the sinews of thy heart?
And when thy heart began to beat,
What dread hand? and what dread feet?

What the hammer? what the chain,
In what furnace was thy brain?
What the anvil? what dread grasp,
Dare its deadly terrors clasp!

When the stars threw down their spears
And water'd heaven with their tears:
Did he smile his work to see?
Did he who made the Lamb make thee?

Tyger Tyger burning bright,
In the forests of the night:
What immortal hand or eye,
Dare frame thy fearful symmetry?

From A Song to David
Christopher Smart

Strong is the horse upon his speed;
Strong in pursuit the rapid glede,
Which makes at once his game:
Strong the tall ostrich on the ground;
Strong thro' the turbulent profound
Shoots xiphias to his aim.

Strong is the lion – like a coal
His eye-ball – like a bastion's mole
His chest against the foes:
Strong, the gier-eagle on his sail,
Strong against tide, th' enormous whale
Emerges as he goes.

But stronger still, in earth and air,
And in the sea, the man of pray'r;
And far beneath the tide;
And in the seat to faith assign'd,
Where ask is have, where seek is find,
Where knock is open wide.

The Mountain and the Squirrel
Ralph Waldo Emerson

The mountain and the squirrel
Had a quarrel;
And the former called the latter 'Little Prig.'
Bun replied,
'You are doubtless very big;
But all sorts of things and weather
Must be taken in together,
To make up a year
And a sphere.
And I think it no disgrace
To occupy my place.
If I'm not so large as you,
You are not so small as I,
And not half so spry.
I'll not deny you make
A very pretty squirrel track;
Talents differ; all is well and wisely put;
If I cannot carry forests on my back,
Neither can you crack a nut.'

Something Told the Wild Geese
Rachel Field

Something told the wild geese
It was time to go.
Though the fields lay golden
Something whispered – 'Snow.'

Leaves were green and stirring,
Berries, lustre-glossed,
But beneath warm feathers
Something cautioned – 'Frost.'

All the sagging orchards
Steamed with amber spice,
But each wild breast stiffened
At remembered ice.

Something told the wild geese
It was time to fly,
Summer sun was on their wings,
Winter in their cry.

The Frog
Hilaire Belloc

Be kind and tender to the Frog,
    And do not call him names,
As 'Slimy skin,' or 'Polly-wog,'
    Or likewise 'Ugly James,'
Or 'Gape-a-grin,' or 'Toad-gone-wrong,'
    Or 'Billy Bandy-knees':
The Frog is justly sensitive
    To epithets like these.
No animal will more repay
    A treatment kind and fair;
At least so lonely people say
Who keep a frog (and, by the way,
They are extremely rare).

The Owl and the Pussy-Cat
Edward Lear

The Owl and the Pussy-cat went to sea
   In a beautiful pea-green boat,
They took some honey, and plenty of money,
   Wrapped up in a five-pound note.
The Owl looked up to the stars above,
   And sang to a small guitar,
'O lovely Pussy! O Pussy, my love,
   What a beautiful Pussy you are,
      You are,
      You are!
What a beautiful Pussy you are!'

Pussy said to the Owl, 'You elegant fowl!
   How charmingly sweet you sing!
O let us be married! too long we have tarried:
   But what shall we do for a ring?'
They sailed away, for a year and a day,
   To the land where the Bong-Tree grows
And there in a wood a Piggy-wig stood
   With a ring at the end of his nose,
      His nose,
   His nose,
With a ring at the end of his nose.

'Dear Pig, are you willing to sell for one shilling
   Your ring?' Said the Piggy, 'I will.'
So they took it away, and were married next day
   By the Turkey who lives on the hill.

They dined on mince, and slices of quince,
   Which they ate with a runcible spoon;
And hand in hand, on the edge of the sand,
   They danced by the light of the moon,
      The moon,
      The moon,
They danced by the light of the moon.

The Donkey
G. K. Chesterton

When fishes flew and forests walked
    And figs grew upon thorn,
Some moment when the moon was blood
    Then surely I was born.

With monstrous head and sickening cry
    And ears like errant wings,
The devil's walking parody
    On all four-footed things.

The tattered outlaw of the earth,
    Of ancient crooked will;
Starve, scourge, deride me: I am dumb,
    I keep my secret still.

Fools! For I also had my hour;
    One far fierce hour and sweet:
There was a shout about my ears,
    And palms before my feet.

Four Feet
Rudyard Kipling

I have done mostly what most men do,
And pushed it out of my mind;
But I can't forget, if I wanted to,
Four-Feet trotting behind.

Day after day, the whole day through–
Wherever my road inclined–
Four-Feet said, 'I am coming with you!'
And trotted along behind.

Now I must go by some other round,–
Which I shall never find–
Somewhere that does not carry the sound
Of Four-Feet trotting behind.

Jim
Hilaire Belloc

There was a Boy whose name was Jim;
His Friends were very good to him.
They gave him Tea, and Cakes, and Jam,
And slices of delicious Ham,
And Chocolate with pink inside
And little Tricycles to ride,
They read him Stories through and through,
And even took him to the Zoo—
But there it was the awful Fate
Befell him, which I now relate.

You know – at least you ought to know,
For I have often told you so –
That Children never are allowed
To leave their Nurses in a Crowd;
Now this was Jim's especial Foible
He ran away when he was able,
And on this inauspicious day
He slipped his hand and ran away!

He hadn't gone a yard when – BANG
With open Jaws, a lion sprang,
And hungrily began to eat
The Boy, beginning at his feet.
Now, just imagine how it feels
When first your toes and then your heels,
And then by gradual degrees,
Your shins and ankles, calves and knees,

Are slowly eaten bit by bit.
No wonder Jim detested it!
No wonder that he shouted 'Hi!'

The Honest Keeper heard his cry,
Though very fat he almost ran
To help the little gentleman.
'Ponto!' he ordered as he came
(For Ponto was the Lion's name)
'Ponto!' he cried, with angry Frown,
'Let go, Sir! Down, Sir! Put it down!'
The Lion made a sudden stop,
He let the Dainty Morsel drop,
And slunk reluctant to his Cage,
Snarling with Disappointed Rage.
But when he bent him over Jim,
The Honest Keeper's eyes grew dim.
The Lion having reached his Head,
The Miserable Boy was dead!

When Nurse informed his Parents, they
Were more concerned than I can say—
His Mother, as she dried her eyes,
Said, 'Well – it gives me no surprise,
He would not do as he was told!'
His Father, who was self-controlled,
Bade all the children round attend
To James's miserable end,
And always keep a-hold of Nurse
For fear of finding something worse.

Jabberwocky
Lewis Carroll

'Twas brillig, and the slithy toves
    Did gyre and gimble in the wabe:
All mimsy were the borogoves,
    And the mome raths outgrabe.

'Beware the Jabberwock, my son!
    The jaws that bite, the claws that catch!
Beware the Jubjub bird, and shun
    The frumious Bandersnatch!'

He took his vorpal sword in hand;
    Long time the manxome foe he sought—
So rested he by the Tumtum tree
    And stood awhile in thought.

And, as in uffish thought he stood,
    The Jabberwock, with eyes of flame,
Came whiffling through the tulgey wood,
    And burbled as it came!

One, two! One, two! And through and through
    The vorpal blade went snicker-snack!
He left it dead, and with its head
    He went galumphing back.

'And hast thou slain the Jabberwock?
    Come to my arms, my beamish boy!
O frabjous day! Callooh! Callay!'
    He chortled in his joy.

'Twas brillig, and the slithy toves
    Did gyre and gimble in the wabe:
All mimsy were the borogoves,
    And the mome raths outgrabe.

Everyone Sang
Siegfried Sassoon

Everyone suddenly burst out singing;
And I was filled with such delight
As prisoned birds must find in freedom,
Winging wildly across the white
Orchards and dark-green fields; on – on – and out of
      sight.

Everyone's voice was suddenly lifted;
And beauty came like the setting sun:
My heart was shaken with tears; and horror
Drifted away … O, but Everyone
Was a bird; and the song was wordless; the singing
      will never be done.

Love

The Bargain
Sir Philip Sidney

My true-love hath my heart, and I have his,
   By just exchange one for another given:
I hold his dear, and mine he cannot miss,
    There never was a better bargain driven.
       My true-love hath my heart, and I have his.

His heart in me keeps me and him in one,
   My heart in him his thoughts and senses guides:
He loves my heart, for once it was his own,
    I cherish his because in me it bides:
       My true-love hath my heart, and I have his.

Annabel Lee
Edgar Allan Poe

It was many and many a year ago,
    In a kingdom by the sea,
That a maiden there lived whom you may know
    By the name of Annabel Lee;
And this maiden she lived with no other thought
    Than to love and be loved by me.

I was a child and *she* was a child
    In this kingdom by the sea,
But we loved with a love that was more than love–
    I and my Annabel Lee–
With a love that the wingèd seraphs of Heaven
    Coveted her and me.

And this was the reason that, long ago,
    In this kingdom by the sea,
A wind blew out of a cloud, chilling
    My beautiful Annabel Lee;
So that her highborn kinsmen came
    And bore her away from me,
To shut her up in a sepulchre
    In this kingdom by the sea.

The angels, not half so happy in Heaven,
    Went envying her and me–
Yes! – that was the reason (as all men know,
    In this kingdom by the sea)
That the wind came out of the cloud by night,
    Chilling and killing my Annabel Lee.

But our love it was stronger by far than the love
   Of those who were older than we—
   Of many far wiser than we—
And neither the angels in Heaven above,
   Nor the demons down under the sea,
Can ever dissever my soul from the soul
   Of the beautiful Annabel Lee.

For the moon never beams, without bringing me
      dreams
   Of the beautiful Annabel Lee;
And the stars never rise, but I feel the bright eyes
   Of the beautiful Annabel Lee;
And so, all the night-tide, I lie down by the side
   Of my darling – my darling – my life and my bride,
   In the sepulchre there by the sea –
   In her tomb by the sounding sea.

Bessie's Song to her Doll
Lewis Carroll

Matilda Jane, you never look
At any toy or picture-book.
I show you pretty things in vain —
You must be blind, Matilda Jane!

I ask you riddles, tell you tales,
But *all* our conversation fails.
You *never* answer me again —
I fear you're dumb, Matilda Jane!

Matilda darling, when I call,
You never seem to hear at all.
I shout with all my might and main —
But you're *so* deaf, Matilda Jane!

Matilda Jane, you needn't mind,
For, though you're deaf and dumb and blind,
There's *some one* loves you, it is plain—
And that is *me*, Matilda Jane!

Carpe Diem
Laurence Hope

And if fate remember later, and come to claim her
>   due,
What sorrow would be greater than the joy I shared
>   with you,
For today lit by laughter, between the crushing
>   years,
I will chance in the hereafter, eternities of tears!

Eros
Ralph Waldo Emerson

The sense of the world is short,–
Long and various the report,–
   To love and be beloved;
Men and gods have not outlearned it;
And, how oft soe'er they've turned it,
   'Tis not to be improved.

I am only the house of your beloved
Rumi

'I am only the house of your beloved,
not the beloved herself:
true love is for the treasure,
not for the coffer that contains it.'
The real beloved is that one who is unique,
who is your beginning and your end.
When you find that one,
you'll no longer expect anything else:
that is both the manifest and the mystery.
That one is the lord of states of feeling,
dependent on none;
month and year are slaves to that moon.
When he bids the 'state,'
It does His bidding;
When that one wills, bodies become spirit.

Bonnie Charlie
Lady Nairne

Bonnie Charlie's noo awa
Safely o'er the friendly main;
He'rts will a'most break in twa
Should he no' come back again.

Will ye no' come back again?
Will ye no' come back again?
Better lo'ed ye canna be
Will ye no' come back again?

Ye trusted in your Hieland men
They trusted you, dear Charlie;
They kent you hiding in the glen,
Your cleadin' was but barely.

English bribes were a' in vain
An 'e'en tho puirer we may be
Siller canna buy the heart
That beats aye for thine and thee.

We watch'd thee in the gloamin' hour
We watch'd thee in the mornin' grey
Tho' thirty thousand pound they'd gi'e
Oh, there is nane that wad betray.

Sweet's the laverock's note and lang,
Liltin' wildly up the glen,
But aye to me he sings ane sang,
Will ye no come back again?

Aedh Wishes for the Cloths of Heaven
William Butler Yeats

Had I the heavens' embroidered cloths,
Enwrought with golden and silver light,
The blue and the dim and the dark cloths
Of night and light and the half light,
I would spread the cloths under your feet:
But I, being poor, have only my dreams;
I have spread my dreams under your feet;
Tread softly because you tread on my dreams.

Remember
Christina Rossetti

Remember me when I am gone away,
Gone far away into the silent land;
    When you can no more hold me by the hand,
    Nor I half turn to go yet turning stay.
Remember me when no more day by day
You tell me of our future that you plann'd:
    Only remember me; you understand
    It will be late to counsel then or pray.
Yet if you should forget me for a while
And afterwards remember, do not grieve:
    For if the darkness and corruption leave
    A vestige of the thoughts that once I had,
    Better by far you should forget and smile
Than that you should remember and be sad.

Y'sod, adapted from Ba'al Shem Tov

From every human being there rises a light that
> reaches straight to Heaven.

And when two souls that are destined to be together
find each other,
their streams of light flow together
and a single brighter light goes forth
from their united being.

The Gift of Love
Robert Burns

The Tides of love shall beat the shore,
The stars fall from the sky;
Yet I will love thee more and more
Until the day I die, my dear,
Until the day I die.

From the *Divine Comedy*
Dante

The love of God, unutterable and perfect,
flows into a pure soul the way light
rushes into a transparent object.

The more love we receive, the more love we shine
        forth;
so that, as we grow clear and open,
the more complete the joy of loving is.

And the more souls who resonate together,
the greater the intensity of their love for,
mirror-like, each soul reflects the other.

Love
R. G. Ingersoll

Love is the magician, the enchanter, that changes worthless things to joy, and makes right royal kings and queens of common clay. It is the perfume of that wondrous flower, the heart, and without that sacred passion, that divine swoon, we are less than beasts; but with it, earth is heaven and we are gods.

Victor Hugo

When two souls, which have sought each other for however long in the throng, have finally found each other, when they have seen that they are matched, are in sympathy and compatible, in a word that they are alike, there is then established for ever between them a union, fiery and pure as they themselves are, a union which begins on earth and continues for ever in heaven. This union is love, true love, such as in truth very few men can conceive of, that love ... whose life comes from devotion and passion, and for which the greatest sacrifices are the sweetest delights.

Paradiso XVIII
Dante

Hearing my comfort's loving voice, I turned
To her, but of the love I then beheld,
Within those holy eyes, I tell not here;

Because I do not trust my power of speech,
Nor could my memory retrace its steps
So far unless Another guided it.

But of that moment this much can be said;
That as I gazed on her my heart was freed
From every kind of longing and desire,

For the Eternal Joy that shone direct
On Beatrice was making me content
With its reflection in her lovely eyes.

Dazzling me with the brilliance of her smile,
She said, 'Now turn away and listen well,
Not only in my eyes is Paradise'.

Courage

& Strength

Invictus
W. E. Henley

Out of the night that covers me,
    Black as the pit from pole to pole,
I thank whatever gods may be
    For my unconquerable soul.

In the fell clutch of circumstance
    I have not winced nor cried aloud.
Under the bludgeonings of chance
    My head is bloody, but unbowed.

Beyond this place of wrath and tears
    Looms but the Horror of the shade,
And yet the menace of the years
    Finds and shall find me unafraid.

It matters not how strait the gate,
    How charged with punishments the scroll,
I am the master of my fate,
    I am the captain of my soul.

I Vow to Thee, My Country
Cecil Spring-Rice

I vow to thee, my country, all earthly things above,
Entire and whole and perfect, the service of my love;
The love that asks no questions, the love that stands
    the test,
That lays upon the altar the dearest and the best;
The love that never falters, the love that pays the
    price,
The love that makes undaunted the final sacrifice.

And there's another country, I've heard of long ago,
Most dear to them that love her, most great to them
    that know;
We may not count her armies, we may not see her
    King;
Her fortress is a faithful heart, her pride is suffering;
And soul by soul and silently her shining bounds
    increase,
And her ways are ways of gentleness, and all her paths
    are peace.

Border Ballad
Sir Walter Scott

March, march, Ettrick and Teviotdale,
   Why the deil dinna ye march forward in order!
March, march, Eskdale and Liddesdale,
   All the Blue Bonnets are bound for the Border.
      Many a banner spread,
      Flutters above your head,
   Many a crest that is famous in story.
      Mount and make ready then,
      Sons of the mountain glen,
   Fight for the Queen and our old Scottish glory.

Come from the hills where your hirsels are grazing,
   Come from the glen of the buck and the roe;
Come to the crag where the beacon is blazing,
   Come with the buckler, the lance, and the bow.
      Trumpets are sounding,
      War-steeds are bounding,
   Stand to your arms, then, and march in good order;
      England shall many a day
      Tell of the bloody fray,
When the Blue Bonnets came over the Border.

The Soldier
Rupert Brooke

If I should die, think only this of me:
    That there's some corner of a foreign field
That is for ever England. There shall be
    In that rich earth a richer dust concealed;
A dust whom England bore, shaped, made aware,
    Gave, once, her flowers to love, her ways to roam,
A body of England's, breathing English air,
    Washed by the rivers, blest by suns of home.

And think, this heart, all evil shed away,
    A pulse in the eternal mind, no less
        Gives somewhere back the thoughts by England given;
Her sights and sounds; dreams happy as her day;
    And laughter, learnt of friends; and gentleness,
        In hearts at peace, under an English heaven.

Jerusalem
William Blake

And did those feet in ancient time
Walk upon England's mountains green:
And was the holy Lamb of God,
On England's pleasant pastures seen!

And did the Countenance Divine,
Shine forth upon our clouded hills?
And was Jerusalem builded here,
Among these dark Satanic Mills?

Bring me my Bow of burning gold:
Bring me my arrows of desire:
Bring me my Spear: O clouds unfold!
Bring me my Chariot of fire!

I will not cease from Mental Fight,
Nor shall my sword sleep in my hand:
Till we have built Jerusalem,
In England's green and pleasant Land.

The Lord is My Shepherd, Psalm 23

The Lord is my shepherd; I shall not want.
He maketh me to lie down in green pastures;
He leadeth me beside the still waters.
He restoreth my soul;
He leadeth me in the paths of righteousness for his
    name's sake.
Yea, though I walk through the valley of the shadow of
    death,
I will fear no evil; for thou art with me;
Thy rod and thy staff they comfort me.
Thou preparest a table before me in the presence of
    mine enemies;
Thou anointest my head with oil; my cup runneth
    over.
Surely goodness and mercy shall follow me all the
    days of my life;
And I will dwell in the house of the Lord for ever.

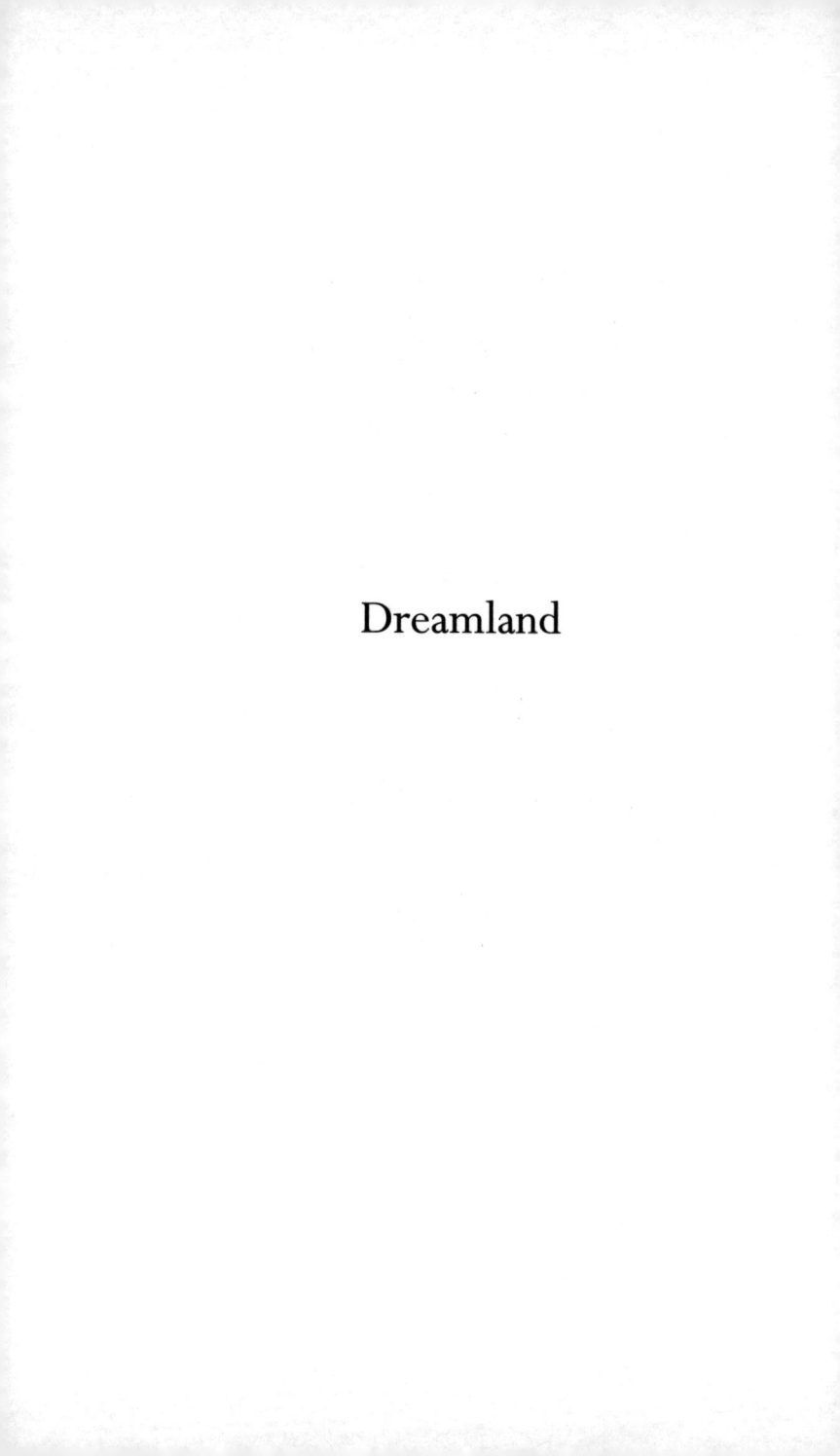

Dreamland

Dreamland
Lewis Carroll

When midnight mists are creeping,
And all the land is sleeping,
Around me tread the mighty dead,
And slowly pass away.
Lo, warriors, saints, and sages,
From out the vanished ages,
With solemn pace and reverend face
Appear and pass away.
The blaze of noonday splendour,
The twilight soft and tender,
May charm the eye: yet they shall die,
Shall die and pass away.
But here, in Dreamland's centre,
No spoiler's hand may enter,
These visions fair, this radiance rare,
Shall never pass away.
I see the shadows falling,
The forms of old recalling;
Around me tread the mighty dead,
And slowly pass away.

From Goblin Market
Christina Rossetti

White and golden Lizzie stood,
Like a lily in a flood,–
Like a rock of blue-veined stone
Lashed by tides obstreperously,–
Like a beacon left alone
In a hoary roaring sea,
Sending up a golden fire,–
Like a fruit-crowned orange-tree
White with blossoms honey-sweet
Sore beset by wasp and bee,–
Like a royal virgin town
Topped with gilded dome and spire
Close beleaguered by a fleet
Mad to tug her standard down.

One may lead a horse to water,
Twenty cannot make him drink.
Though the goblins cuffed and caught her,
Coaxed and fought her,
Bullied and besought her,
Scratched her, pinched her black as ink,
Kicked and knocked her,
Mauled and mocked her,
Lizzie uttered not a word;
Would not open lip from lip
Lest they should cram a mouthful in:
But laughed in heart to feel the drip
Of juice that syrupped all her face,

And lodged in dimples of her chin,
And streaked her neck which quaked like curd.
At last the evil people,
Worn out by her resistance,
Flung back her penny, kicked their fruit
Along whichever road they took,
Not leaving root or stone or shoot;
Some writhed into the ground,
Some dived into the brook
With ring and ripple,
Some scudded on the gale without a sound,
Some vanished in the distance.

Ozymandias
Percy Bysshe Shelley

I met a traveller from an antique land,
Who said: Two vast and trunkless legs of stone
Stand in the desert… Near them, on the sand,
Half sunk a shattered visage lies, whose frown,
And wrinkled lip, and sneer of cold command,
Tell that its sculptor well those passions read
Which yet survive, stamped on these lifeless things,
The hand that mocked them, and the heart that fed;
And on the pedestal, these words appear:
'My name is Ozymandias, King of Kings;
Look on my Works, ye Mighty, and despair!'
Nothing beside remains. Round the decay
Of that colossal Wreck, boundless and bare
The lone and level sands stretch far away.

Christ in the Stranger's Guise
Anon

I met a stranger yester'een;
I put food in the eating place,
Drink in the drinking place,
Music in the listening place;
And, in the sacred name of the Triune,
He blessed myself and my house,
My cattle and my dear ones,
And the lark said in her song,
Often, often, often,
Goes Christ in the stranger's guise;
Often, often, often,
Goes the Christ in the stranger's guise.

Walk a Little Slower, Daddy
Anon

'Walk, a little slower, Daddy' said a little child so small.
'I'm following in your footsteps and I don't want to fall.

Sometimes your steps are very fast,
Sometimes they're hard to see;
So walk a little slower Daddy, for you are leading me.

Someday when I'm all grown up,
You're what I want to be.
Then I will have a little child
Who'll want to follow me.

And I would want to lead just right, and know that I was true;
So, walk a little slower, Daddy, for I must follow you.'

The Courtship of the Yonghy-Bonghy-Bò
Edward Lear

On the Coast of Coromandel
   Where the early pumpkins blow,
      In the middle of the woods
   Lived the Yonghy-Bonghy-Bò.
Two old chairs, and half a candle,–
One old jug without a handle,–
   These were all his worldly goods:
   In the middle of the woods,
   These were all the worldly goods,
Of the Yonghy-Bonghy-Bò,
Of the Yonghy-Bonghy-Bò.

Once, among the Bong-trees walking
   Where the early pumpkins blow,
      To a little heap of stones
   Came the Yonghy-Bonghy-Bò.
There he heard a Lady talking,
To some milk-white Hens of Dorking,–
      ''Tis the lady Jingly Jones!
      'On that little heap of stones
      'Sits the Lady Jingly Jones!'
   Said the Yonghy-Bonghy-Bò,
   Said the Yonghy-Bonghy-Bò.

'Lady Jingly! Lady Jingly!
   'Sitting where the pumpkins blow,
      'Will you come and be my wife?'
   Said the Yonghy-Bonghy-Bò.

'I am tired of living singly,–
'On this coast so wild and shingly,–
    'I'm a-weary of my life:
    'If you'll come and be my wife,
    'Quite serene would be my life!'–
Said the Yonghy-Bonghy-Bò,
Said the Yonghy-Bonghy-Bò.

'On this Coast of Coromandel,
  'Shrimps and watercresses grow,
  'Prawns are plentiful and cheap,'
Said the Yonghy-Bonghy-Bò.
'You shall have my chairs and candle,
'And my jug without a handle!–
    'Gaze upon the rolling deep
    ('Fish is plentiful and cheap)
    'As the sea, my love is deep!'
  Said the Yonghy-Bonghy-Bò,
  Said the Yonghy-Bonghy-Bò.

Lady Jingly answered sadly,
  And her tears began to flow,–
    'Your proposal comes too late,
   'Mr. Yonghy-Bonghy-Bò!
'I would be your wife most gladly!'
(Here she twirled her fingers madly,)
    'But in England I've a mate!
    'Yes! you've asked me far too late,
    'For in England I've a mate,
  'Mr. Yonghy-Bonghy-Bò!
  'Mr. Yonghy-Bonghy-Bò!'

'Mr. Jones – (his name is Handel,–
   'Handel Jones, Esquire, & Co.)
      'Dorking fowls delights to send,
   'Mr. Yonghy-Bonghy-Bò!
'Keep, oh! keep your chairs and candle,
'And your jug without a handle,–
      'I can merely be your friend!
      '– Should my Jones more Dorkings send,
      'I will give you three, my friend!
   'Mr. Yonghy-Bonghy-Bò!
   'Mr. Yonghy-Bonghy-Bò!'

'Though you've such a tiny body,
   'And your head so large doth grow,–
      'Though your hat may blow away,
   'Mr. Yonghy-Bonghy-Bò!
'Though you're such a Hoddy Doddy–
'Yet a wish that I could modi-
      'fy the words I needs must say!
      'Will you please to go away?
   'That is all I have to say–
   'Mr. Yonghy-Bonghy-Bò!
   'Mr. Yonghy-Bonghy-Bò!'

Down the slippery slopes of Myrtle,
   Where the early pumpkins blow,
      To the calm and silent sea
   Fled the Yonghy-Bonghy-Bò.
There, beyond the Bay of Gurtle,
Lay a large and lively Turtle,–
      'You're the Cove,' he said, 'for me

    'On your back beyond the sea,
      'Turtle, you shall carry me!'
Said the Yonghy-Bonghy-Bò,
Said the Yonghy-Bonghy-Bò.

Through the silent-roaring ocean
   Did the Turtle swiftly go;
     Holding fast upon his shell
   Rode the Yonghy-Bonghy-Bò.
With a sad primeval motion
Towards the sunset isles of Boshen
     Still the Turtle bore him well.
     Holding fast upon his shell,
      'Lady Jingly Jones, farewell!'
Sang the Yonghy-Bonghy-Bò,
Sang the Yonghy-Bonghy-Bò.

From the Coast of Coromandel
   Did that Lady never go;
     On that heap of stones she mourns
   For the Yonghy-Bonghy-Bò.
On that Coast of Coromandel,
In his jug without a handle
     Still she weeps, and daily moans;
     On that little heap of stones
    To her Dorking Hens she moans,
   For the Yonghy-Bonghy-Bò,
   For the Yonghy-Bonghy-Bò.

When I Consider How My Light is Spent
John Milton

When I consider how my light is spent,
    Ere half my days, in this dark world and wide,
    And that one Talent which is death to hide
    Lodged with me useless, though my Soul more bent
To serve therewith my Maker, and present
    My true account, lest he returning chide;
    'Doth God exact day-labour, light denied?'
    I fondly ask. But patience, to prevent
That murmur, soon replies, 'God doth not need
    Either man's work or his own gifts; who best
    Bear his mild yoke, they serve him best. His state
Is Kingly. Thousands at his bidding speed
    And post o'er Land and Ocean without rest:
    They also serve who only stand and wait.'

Up-Hill
Christina Rossetti

Does the road wind up-hill all the way?
   Yes, to the very end.
Will the day's journey take the whole long day?
   From morn to night, my friend.

But is there for the night a resting-place?
   A roof for when the slow dark hours begin.
May not the darkness hide it from my face?
   You cannot miss that inn.

Shall I meet other wayfarers at night?
   Those who have gone before.
Then must I knock, or call when just in sight?
   They will not keep you standing at that door.

Shall I find comfort, travel-sore and weak?
   Of labour you shall find the sum.
Will there be beds for me and all who seek?
   Yea, beds for all who come.

The Naughty Brother
Bertie Hughes

Two months ago I shot my brother,
So we went to the shop to buy another.
Annoyingly though they'd sold out.

As his replacement we bought a trout.
My parents even made me pay!
The price of that fish was not OK!
I had a great time with my little trout,
He was as good company as my brother, without a doubt.
I played with my fish for years and years. When it died, I burst into tears.
The moral of this story is that when you shoot your brother you don't get covered in glory.

Brother and Sister
Lewis Carroll

'Sister, sister, go to bed!
Go and rest your weary head.'
Thus the prudent brother said.

'Do you want a battered hide,
Or scratches to your face applied?'
Thus his sister calm replied.

'Sister, do not raise my wrath.
I'd make you into mutton broth
As easily as kill a moth'

The sister raised her beaming eye
And looked on him indignantly
And sternly answered, 'Only try!'

Off to the cook he quickly ran.
'Dear Cook, please lend a frying-pan
To me as quickly as you can.'

'And wherefore should I lend it you?'
'The reason, Cook, is plain to view.
I wish to make an Irish stew.'

'What meat is in that stew to go?'
'My sister'll be the contents!'
'Oh'

'You'll lend the pan to me, Cook?'
'No!'

Moral: Never stew your sister.

A Fairy Went A-Marketing
Rose Fyleman

A fairy went a-marketing

She bought a little fish;
She put it in a crystal bowl

Upon a golden dish.
An hour she sat in wonderment

And watched its silver gleam,
And then she gently took it up

And slipped it in a stream.

A fairy went a-marketing

She bought a coloured bird;
It sang the sweetest, shrillest song

That ever she had heard.
She sat beside its painted cage

And listened half the day,
And then she opened wide the door

And let it fly away.

A fairy went a-marketing

She bought a winter gown
All stitched about with gossamer

And lined with thistledown.
She wore it all the afternoon

With prancing and delight,
Then gave it to a little frog

To keep him warm at night.

A fairy went a-marketing

She bought a gentle mouse
To take her tiny messages,

To keep her tiny house.
All day she kept its busy feet

Pit-patting to and fro,
And then she kissed its silken ears,

Thanked it, and let it go.

Disobedience
A. A. Milne

James James
Morrison Morrison
Weatherby George Dupree
Took great
Care of his Mother,
Though he was only three.
James James Said to his Mother,
'Mother,' he said, said he;
'You must never go down
to the end of the town,
if you don't go down with me.'

James James
Morrison's Mother
Put on a golden gown.
James James Morrison's Mother
Drove to the end of the town.
James James Morrison's Mother
Said to herself, said she:
'I can get right down
to the end of the town
and be back in time for tea.'

King John
Put up a notice,
'LOST or STOLEN or STRAYED!
JAMES JAMES MORRISON'S MOTHER
SEEMS TO HAVE BEEN MISLAID.

LAST SEEN
WANDERING VAGUELY:
QUITE OF HER OWN ACCORD,
SHE TRIED TO GET DOWN
TO THE END OF THE TOWN –
FORTY SHILLINGS REWARD!'

James James
Morrison Morrison
(Commonly known as Jim)
Told his
Other relations
Not to go blaming *him*.
James James
Said to his Mother,
'Mother,' he said, said he:
'You must *never* go down to the end of the town
without consulting me.'

James James
Morrison's mother
Hasn't been heard of since.
King John said he was sorry,
So did the Queen and Prince.
King John
(Somebody told me)
Said to a man he knew:
'If people go down to the end of the town, well,
what can *anyone* do?'

(Now then, very softly)

[63]

J.J.
M.M.
W. G. Du P.
Took great
C/O his M*****
Though he was only 3.
J. J. said to his M*****
'M*****,' he said, said he:
'You-must-never-go-down-to-the-end-of-the-town—
if-you-don't-go-down-with-ME!'

The Natural World

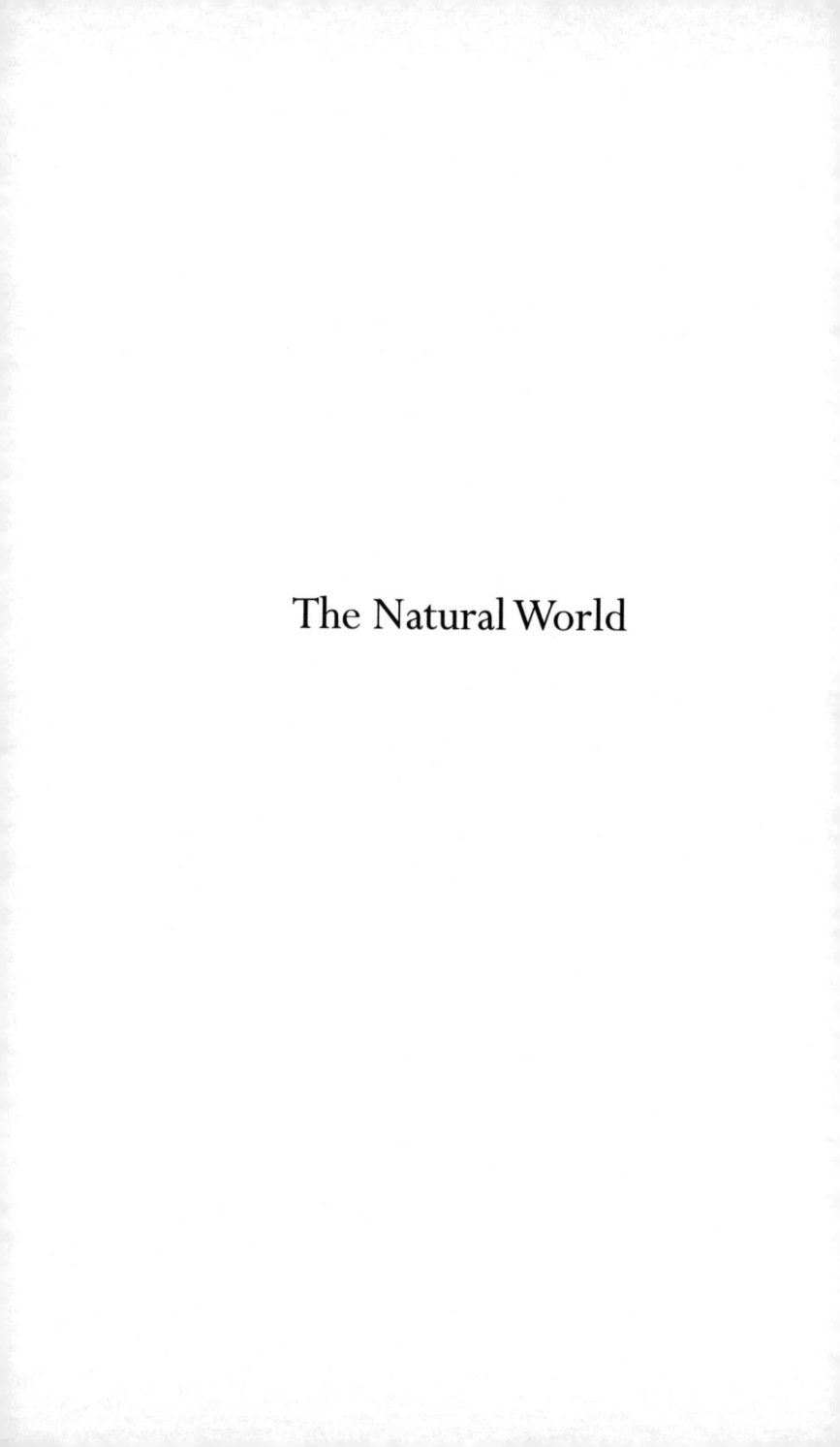

A Charm
Rudyard Kipling

Take of English earth as much
As either hand may rightly clutch.
In the taking of it breathe
Prayer for all who lie beneath.
Not the great nor well-bespoke,
But the mere uncounted folk
Of whose life and death is none
Report or lamentation.
    Lay that earth upon thy heart,
    And thy sickness shall depart!

It shall sweeten and make whole
Fevered breath and festered soul.
It shall mightily restrain
Over-busied hand and brain.
It shall ease thy mortal strife
'Gainst the immortal woe of life,
Till thyself, restored, shall prove
By what grace the Heavens do move.

Take of English flowers these—
Spring's full-faced primroses,
Summer's wild wide-hearted rose,
Autumn's wall-flower of the close,
And, thy darkness to illume,
Winter's bee-thronged ivy-bloom.
Seek and serve them where they bide
From Candlemas to Christmas-tide,

    For these simples, used aright,
    Can restore a failing sight.

These shall cleanse and purify
Webbed and inward-turning eye;
These shall show thee treasure hid
Thy familiar fields amid;
And reveal (which is thy need)
Every man a King indeed!

The Fairies
William Allingham

Up the airy mountain,
Down the rushy glen,
We daren't go a-hunting
For fear of little men;
Wee folk, good folk,
Trooping all together;
Green jacket, red cap,
And white owl's feather!

Down along the rocky shore
Some make their home,
They live on crispy pancakes
Of yellow tide-foam;
Some in the reeds
Of the black mountain lake,
With frogs for their watch-dogs,
All night awake.

High on the hill-top
The old King sits;
He is now so old and grey
He's nigh lost his wits.
With a bridge of white mist
Columbkill he crosses,
On his stately journeys
From Slieveleague to Rosses;
Or going up with music
On cold starry nights

To sup with the Queen
Of the gay Northern Lights.

They stole little Bridget
For seven years long;
When she came down again
Her friends were all gone.
They took her lightly back,
Between the night and morrow,
They thought that she was fast asleep,
But she was dead with sorrow.
They have kept her ever since
Deep within the lake,
On a bed of fig-leaves,
Watching till she wake.

By the craggy hill-side,
Through the mosses bare,
They have planted thorn trees
For my pleasure, here and there.
Is any man so daring
As dig them up in spite,
He shall find their sharpest thorns
In his bed at night.

Up the airy mountain,
Down the rushy glen,
We daren't go a-hunting
For fear of little men;
Wee folk, good folk,

Trooping all together;
Green jacket, red cap,
And white owl's feather!

Snowdrops
Mary Vivian

I like to think
That, long ago,
There fell to earth
Some flakes of snow
Which loved this cold,
Grey world of ours
So much, they stayed
As snowdrop flowers.

From Sir Galahad
Alfred, Lord Tennyson

Sometimes on lonely mountain-meres
I find a magic bark;
I leap on board; no helmsman steers;
I float till all is dark.
A gentle sound, an awful light!
Three angels bear the holy Grail;
With folded feet, in stoles of white,
On sleeping wings they sail.
Ah, blessed vision! blood of God!
My spirit beats her mortal bars,
As down dark tides the glory slides,
And star-like mingles with the stars.

The Stolen Child
William Butler Yeats

Where dips the rocky highland
Of Sleuth Wood in the lake,
There lies a leafy island
Where flapping herons wake
The drowsy water rats;
There we've hid our faery vats,
Full of berries
And of reddest stolen cherries.

Come away, O human child!
To the waters and the wild
With a faery, hand in hand.
For the world's more full of weeping
Than you can understand.

Where the wave of moonlight glosses
The dim grey sands with light,
Far off by furthest Rosses
We foot it all the night,
Weaving olden dances
Mingling hands and mingling glances
Till the moon has taken flight;
To and fro we leap
And chase the frothy bubbles,
While the world is full of troubles
And is anxious in its sleep.

Come away, O human child!
To the waters and the wild
With a faery, hand in hand,
For the world's more full of weeping
Than you can understand.

Where the wandering water gushes
From the hills above Glen-Car,
In pools among the rushes
That scarce could bathe a star,
We seek for slumbering trout
And whispering in their ears
Give them unquiet dreams;
Leaning softly out
From ferns that drop their tears
Over the young streams.

Come away, O human child!
To the waters and the wild
With a faery, hand in hand,
For the world's more full of weeping
Than you can understand.

Away with us he's going,
The solemn-eyed:
He'll hear no more the lowing
Of the calves on the warm hillside
Or the kettle on the hob
Sing peace into his breast,

Or see the brown mice bob
Round and round the oatmeal chest.

For he comes, the human child,
To the waters and the wild
With a faery, hand in hand,
For the world's more full of weeping
Than he can understand.

Windy Nights
Robert Louis Stevenson

Whenever the moon and stars are set,
Whenever the wind is high,
All night long in the dark and wet,
A man goes riding by.
Late in the night when the fires are out,
Why does he gallop and gallop about?

Whenever the trees are crying aloud,
And ships are tossed at sea,
By, on the highway, low and loud,
By at the gallop goes he.
By at the gallop he goes, and then
By he comes back at the gallop again.

I Thank Thee, God, That I Have Lived
Elizabeth Craven

I thank thee God, that I have lived
In this great world and known its many joys:
The songs of birds, the strongest sweet scent of hay,
And cooling breezes in the secret dusk;
The flaming sunsets at the close of day,
Hills and the lovely, heather-covered moors;
Music at night, and the moonlight on the sea,
The beat of waves upon the rocky shore
And wild white spray, flung high in ecstasy;
The faithful eyes of dogs, and treasured books,
The love of Kin and fellowship of friends
And all that makes life dear and beautiful.

I thank Thee too, that there has come to me
A little sorrow and sometimes defeat,
A little heartache and the loneliness
That comes with parting and the words 'Good-bye';
Dawn breaking after weary hours of pain,
When I discovered that night's gloom must yield
And morning light break through to me again.
Because of these and other blessings poured
Unasked upon my wondering head,
Because I know that there is yet to come
An even richer and more glorious life,
And most of all, because Thine only Son
Once sacrificed life's loveliness for me,
I thank Thee, God, that I have lived.

Past, Present, Future
Emily Brontë

Tell me, tell me, smiling child,
What the past is like to thee?
'An Autumn evening soft and mild
With a wind that sighs mournfully.'

Tell me, what is the present hour?
'A green and flowery spray
Where a young bird sits gathering its power
To mount and fly away.'

And what is the future, happy one?
'A sea beneath a cloudless sun;
A mighty, glorious, dazzling sea
Stretching into infinity.'

The Song of the River
William Randolph Hearst

The snow melts on the mountain
And the water runs down to the spring,
And the spring in a turbulent fountain,
With a song of youth to sing,
Runs down to the riotous river,
And the river flows to the sea,
And the water again
Goes back in rain
To the hills where it used to be.
And I wonder if life's deep mystery
Isn't much like the rain and the snow
Returning through all eternity
To the places it used to know.

For life was born on the lofty heights
And flows in a laughing stream
To the river below
Whose onward flow
Ends in a peaceful dream.
And so at last,
When our life has passed
And the river has run its course,
It again goes back,
O'er the selfsame track,
To the mountain which was its source.

So why prize life
Or why fear death,
Or dread what is to be?
The river ran its allotted span
Till it reached the silent sea.
Then the water harked back to the mountaintop
To begin its course once more.
So we shall run the course begun
Till we reach the silent shore,
Then revisit earth in a pure rebirth
From the heart of the virgin snow.
So don't ask why we live or die,
Or whither, or when we go,
Or wonder about the mysteries
That only God may know.

From Paradise Lost
John Milton

With thee conversing I forget all time;
All seasons, and their change, all please alike.
Sweet is the breath of Morn, her rising sweet,
With charm of earliest birds; pleasant the sun
When first on this delightful land he spreads
His orient beams, on herb, tree, fruit, and flower,
Glistering with dew; fragrant the fertile earth
After soft showers; and sweet the coming on
Of grateful Evening mild; then silent Night
With this her solemn bird, and this fair moon,
And these the gems of Heaven, her starry train:
But neither breath of Morn when she ascends
With charm of earliest birds; nor rising sun
On this delightful land, nor herb, fruit, flower,
Glistering with dew; nor fragrance after showers;
Nor grateful Evening mild, nor silent Night,
With this her solemn bird, nor walk by moon,
Or glittering star-light, without thee is sweet.

Why God Made Little Boys
Anon

God made a world out of His dreams,
Of magic mountains, oceans and streams,
Prairies and plains and wooded land,
Then paused and thought 'I need someone to stand
On top of the mountains, to conquer the seas,
Explore the plains and climb the trees.
Someone to start out small and grow,
Sturdy, strong as a tree…' And so,
He created boys, full of spirit and fun,
To explore and conquer, to romp and run.
With dirty faces and banged up chins,
With courageous hearts and boyish grins.
When He had completed the task He'd begun
He surely said 'A job well done'.

Guidance

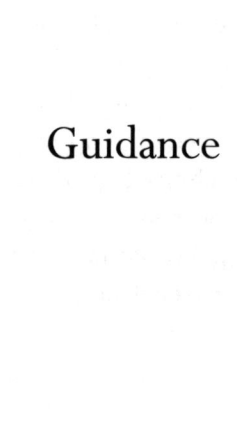

If
Rudyard Kipling

If you can keep your head when all about you
    Are losing theirs and blaming it on you,
If you can trust yourself when all men doubt you,
    But make allowance for their doubting too;
If you can wait and not be tired by waiting,
    Or being lied about, don't deal in lies,
Or being hated, don't give way to hating,
    And yet don't look too good, nor talk too wise:

If you can dream – and not make dreams your master;
    If you can think – and not make thoughts your aim;
If you can meet with Triumph and Disaster
    And treat those two impostors just the same;
If you can bear to hear the truth you've spoken
    Twisted by knaves to make a trap for fools,
Or watch the things you gave your life to, broken,
    And stoop and build 'em up with worn-out tools:

If you can make one heap of all your winnings
    And risk it on one turn of pitch-and-toss,
And lose, and start again at your beginnings
    And never breathe a word about your loss;
If you can force your heart and nerve and sinew
    To serve your turn long after they are gone,
And so hold on when there is nothing in you
    Except the Will which says to them: 'Hold on!'

If you can talk with crowds and keep your virtue,
    Or walk with Kings – nor lose the common touch,
If neither foes nor loving friends can hurt you,
    If all men count with you, but none too much;
If you can fill the unforgiving minute
    With sixty seconds' worth of distance run,
Yours is the Earth and everything that's in it,
    And – which is more – you'll be a Man, my son!

Sonnet 94
William Shakespeare

They that have power to hurt and will do none,
That do not do the thing they most do show,
Who, moving others, are themselves as stone,
Unmoved, cold, and to temptation slow;
They rightly do inherit heaven's graces
And husband nature's riches from expense;
They are the lords and owners of their faces,
Others but stewards of their excellence.
The summer's flower is to the summer sweet,
Though to itself it only live and die,
But if that flower with base infection meet,
The basest weed outbraves his dignity;
    For sweetest things turn sourest by their deeds;
    Lilies that fester smell far worse than weeds.

Wisdom
Laurence Hope

For this is Wisdom; to love, to live
To take what Fate, or the Gods, may give.
To ask no question, to make no prayer,
To kiss the lips and caress the hair,
Speed passion's ebb as you greet its flow,
To have, – to hold – and – in time, – let go!

The New Colossus
Emma Lazarus

Not like the brazen giant of Greek fame,
With conquering limbs astride from land to land;
Here at our sea-washed, sunset gates shall stand
A mighty woman with a torch, whose flame
Is the imprisoned lightning, and her name
Mother of Exiles. From her beacon-hand
Glows world-wide welcome; her mild eyes command
The air-bridged harbor that twin cities frame.
'Keep, ancient lands, your storied pomp!' cries she
With silent lips. 'Give me your tired, your poor,
Your huddled masses yearning to breathe free,
The wretched refuse of your teeming shore.
Send these, the homeless, tempest-tost to me,
I lift my lamp beside the golden door!'

Man's Testament
Adam Lindsay Gordon

Question not, but live and labour
Till yon goal be won,
Helping every feeble neighbour,
Seeking help from none;
Life is mostly froth and bubble,
Two things stand like stone,
Kindness in another's trouble,
Courage in your own.

Happy The Man
John Dryden

Happy the man, and happy he alone,
He who can call today his own:
He who, secure within, can say,
Tomorrow do thy worst, for I have lived today.
Be fair or foul or rain or shine,
The joys I have possessed, in spite of fate, are mine.
Not Heaven itself upon the past has power,
But what has been, has been, and I have had my hour.

The Cry-Baby
Heinrich Hoffmann

'Oh, why are you always so bitterly crying?
You surely will make yourself blind.
What reason on earth for such sobbing and sighing,
I pray, can you possibly find?
There is no real sorrow, there's nothing distressing,
To make you thus grieve and lament.
Ah! no; you are just at this moment possessing
Whatever should make you content.

Now do, my dear daughter, give over this weeping,'
Such was a kind mother's advice.
But all was in vain; for you see she's still keeping
Her handkerchief up to her eyes.

But now she removes it, and oh! she discloses
A countenance full of dismay;
For she certainly feels, or at least she supposes
Her eyesight is going away.
She is not mistaken, her sight is departing;
She knows it and sorrows the more;
Then rubs her sore eyes, to relieve them from
        smarting,
And makes them still worse than before.

And now the poor creature is cautiously crawling
And feeling her way all around;
And now from their sockets her eyeballs are falling;
See, there they are down on the ground.

My children, from such an example take warning,
And happily live while you may;
And say to yourselves, when you rise in the morning,
'I'll try to be cheerful today.'

Ithaka
C. P. Cavafy

As you set out for Ithaka
hope your road is a long one,
full of adventure, full of discovery.
Laistrygonians, Cyclops,
angry Poseidon – don't be afraid of them:
you'll never find things like that on your way
as long as you keep your thoughts raised high,
as long as a rare excitement
stirs your spirit and your body.
Laistrygonians, Cyclops,
wild Poseidon – you won't encounter them
unless you bring them along inside your soul,
unless your soul sets them up in front of you.

Hope your road is a long one.
May there be many summer mornings when,
with what pleasure, what joy,
you enter harbours you're seeing for the first time;
may you stop at Phoenician trading stations
to buy fine things,
mother of pearl and coral, amber and ebony,
sensual perfume of every kind—
as many sensual perfumes as you can;
and may you visit many Egyptian cities
to learn and go on learning from their scholars.

Keep Ithaka always in your mind.
Arriving there is what you're destined for.

But don't hurry the journey at all.
Better if it lasts for years,
so you're old by the time you reach the island,
wealthy with all you've gained on the way,
not expecting Ithaka to make you rich.

Ithaka gave you the marvellous journey.
Without her you wouldn't have set out.
She has nothing left to give you now.

And if you find her poor, Ithaka won't have fooled
      you.
Wise as you will have become, so full of experience,
you'll have understood by then what these Ithakas
      mean.

Historical

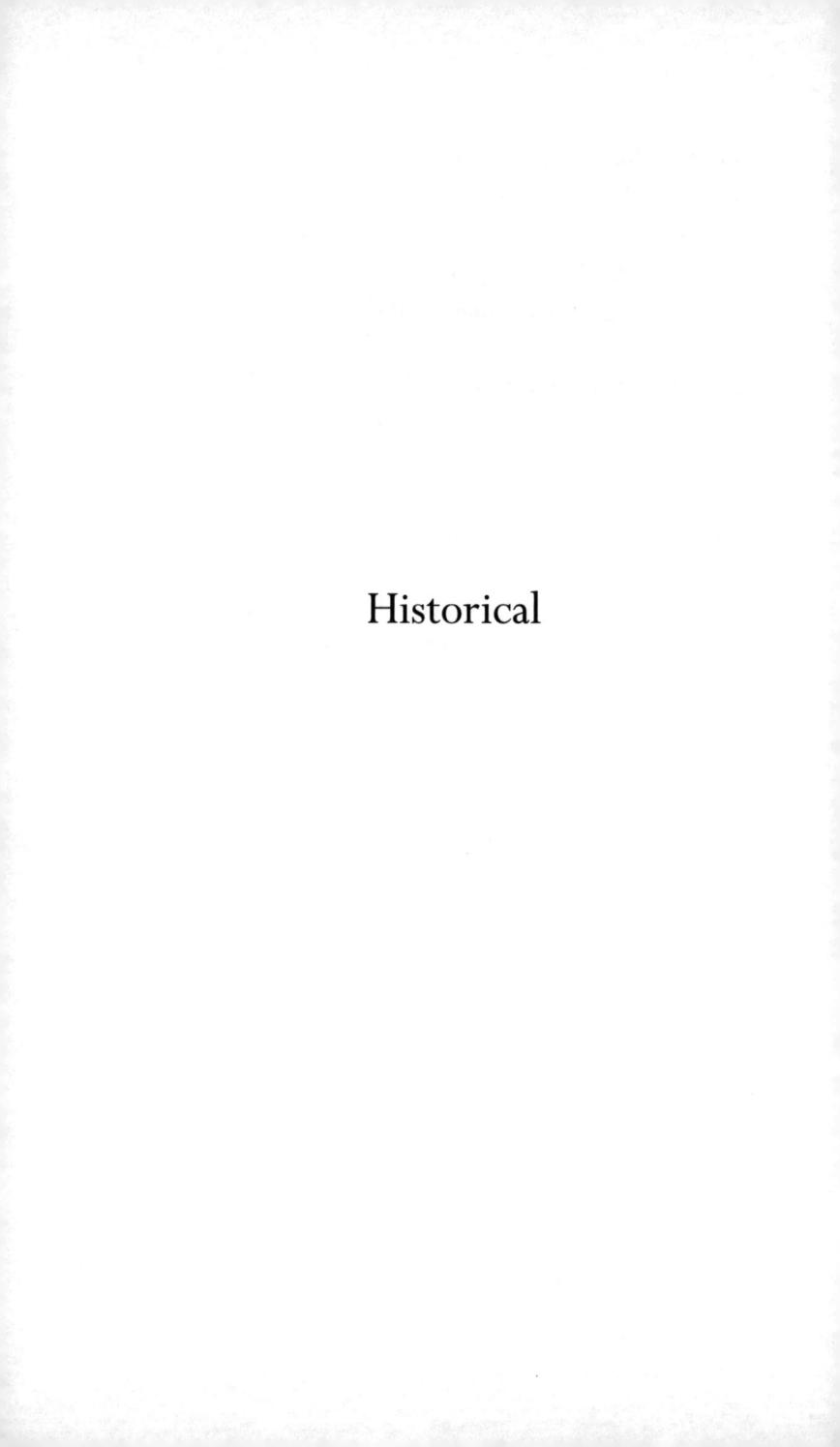

John of Gaunt's dying speech
From Richard II

This royal throne of kings, this scepter'd isle,
This earth of majesty, this seat of Mars,
This other Eden, demi-paradise,
This fortress built by Nature for herself
Against infection and the hand of war,
This happy breed of men, this little world,
This precious stone set in the silver sea,
Which serves it in the office of a wall,
Or as a moat defensive to a house,
Against the envy of less happier lands,
This blessed plot, this earth, this realm, this England,
This nurse, this teeming womb of royal kings,
Fear'd by their breed and famous by their birth,
Renowned for their deeds as far from home,
For Christian service and true chivalry,
As is the sepulchre in stubborn Jewry,
Of the world's ransom, blessed Mary's Son,
This land of such dear souls, this dear dear land…

Queen Elizabeth I's Speech at Tilbury

'My loving people, We have been persuaded by some that are careful of our safety, to take heed how we commit ourselves to armed multitudes, for fear of treachery; but I assure you I do not desire to live to distrust my faithful and loving people.

Let tyrants fear. I have always so behaved myself that, under God, I have placed my chiefest strength and safeguard in the loyal hearts and good-will of my subjects; and therefore I am come amongst you, as you see, at this time, not for my recreation and disport, but being resolved, in the midst and heat of the battle, to live and die amongst you all; to lay down for my God, and for my kingdom, and my people, my honour and my blood, even in the dust.

I know I have the body of a weak, feeble woman; but I have the heart and stomach of a king, and of a king of England too, and think foul scorn that Parma or Spain, or any prince of Europe, should dare to invade the borders of my realm; to which rather than any dishonour shall grow by me, I myself will take up arms, I myself will be your general, judge, and rewarder of every one your virtues in the field.

I know already, for your forwardness you have deserved rewards and crowns; and We do assure you on a word of a prince, they shall be duly paid. In the mean time, my lieutenant general shall be in my stead, than whom never prince commanded a more noble or worthy subject; not doubting but by your obedience to my general, by your concord in the camp, and your valour in the field, we shall shortly have a famous victory over these enemies of my God, of my kingdom, and of my people.'

Queen Elizabeth I's Golden Speech

'Mr Speaker, we perceive your coming is to present thanks to us.

Know that I accept them with no less joy than your loves can have desire to offer such a present, and do more esteem it than any treasure or riches; for those we know how to prize, but loyalty, love and thanks, I account them invaluable.

And though God hath raised me high, yet this I account the glory of my crown, that I have reigned with your loves. This makes me that I do not so much rejoice that God hath made me to be a Queen, as to be a Queen over so thankful a people, and to be the means under God to conserve you in safety and to preserve you from danger.

It is not my desire to live or reign longer than my life and reign shall be for your good. And though you have had, and may have, many mightier and wiser princes sitting in this seat, yet you never had, nor shall have, any that will love you better.'

Prayers

Gaelic Blessing

May the road rise up to meet you,
May the wind be always at your back,
May the sun shine warm upon your face,
The rains fall soft upon your fields,
And until we meet again,
May God hold you in the palm of his hand.

Serenity Prayer
Reinhold Niebuhr

God grant me the serenity to accept the things
        I cannot change,
Courage to change the things I can,
And the wisdom to know the difference.

Gentle Jesus, Meek and Mild
Charles Wesley

Gentle Jesus, meek and mild,
Look upon a little child;
Pity my simplicity,
And suffer me to come to Thee.

Matthew, Mark, Luke and John

Matthew, Mark, Luke and John;
Bless the bed that I lie on.
Four corners to my bed,
Four angels round it spread,
One to watch and one to pray
And two to bear my soul away.

Saint Francis of Assisi

Lord, make me an instrument of Your peace;
Where there is hatred, let me sow love;
Where there is injury, pardon;
Where there is error, truth;
Where there is doubt, faith;
Where there is despair, hope;
Where there is darkness, light;
And where there is sadness, joy.
O Divine Master;
Grant that I may not so much seek
To be consoled as to console;
To be understood as to understand;
To be loved as to love
For it is in giving that we receive;
It is in pardoning that we are pardoned;
It is in dying that we are born to eternal life.

A Child's Prayer on Waking

Now I wake and see the light,
Your love was with me
All through the night;
To You I speak again and pray
That You will lead me all the day.
Amen.

Blessing for a Home, a traditional Jewish blessing

Let no sadness
come through this gate,
Let no trouble
come to this dwelling,
Let no fear come
through this door,
Let no conflict
be in this place,
Let this home be filled
with the blessing of joy
and peace.

The Supplication of Light,
an Islamic prayer

O God,
Place light in my heart,
light on my tongue,
light in my hearing,
light in my sight,
light behind me,
light in front of me,
light on my right,
light on my left,
light above me, and light below me;
place light in my sinew,
in my flesh,
in my blood, in my hair, and in my skin;
place light in my soul
and make light abundant for me;
make me light and grant me light.

A Child's Bedtime Prayer

Now I lay me down to sleep,
I pray You, Lord,
My soul to keep;
Your love stay with me
through the night
and wake me
with the morning light.
Amen.

'Where I sit is holy...'

Where I sit is holy,
Holy is the ground
Forest, mountain, river,
Listen to the sound.
Great Spirit circle
All around me.

Beloved Lord
Hazrat Inayat Khan

Beloved Lord, Almighty God!
Through the rays of the sun,
Through the waves of the air,
Through the All-pervading Life in space,
Purify and revivify me, and, I pray,
Heal my body, heart, and soul.
Amen.

'As We Are Together…'
Thich Nhat Hanh

As we are together, praying for peace, let us be truly with each other.
Let us pay attention to our breathing.
Let us be relaxed in our bodies and our minds.
Let us be at peace with our bodies and our minds.
Let us return to ourselves and become wholly ourselves. Let us maintain a half smile on our faces.
Let us be aware of the source of being common to us all and to all living things.
Evoking the presence of the Great Compassion. Let us fill our hearts with our own compassion, towards ourselves and towards all living beings.
Let us pray that all living beings realise that they are all brothers and sisters,
All nourished from the same source of life.
Let us pray that we ourselves cease to be the cause of suffering to each other.
Let us plead with ourselves to live in a way which will not deprive other beings of air, water, food, shelter, or the chance to live.
With humility, with awareness of the existence of life, and of the sufferings that are going on around us, let us pray for the establishment of peace in our hearts and on earth.
Amen.

I see the moon, and the moon sees me
God bless the moon and God bless me.

Irish Blessing

May you always have walls for the winds,
A roof for the rain,
Tea beside the fire,
Laughter to cheer you, those you love near you,
And all your heart might desire.

May the sun shine all day long,
Everything go right, and nothing go wrong.
May those you love bring love back to you,
And may all the wishes you wish come true.

May luck be your friend
In whatever you do
And may trouble be always
a stranger to you.

In life, there are an infinite number of doors.
If you are diligent, you will open some of them.
If you are brilliant, you will open many of them.
But if you are vibrant, they will open for you.

Marianne Williamson

'Our deepest fear is not that we are inadequate. Our deepest fear is that we are powerful beyond measure. It is our light, not our darkness that most frightens us. We ask ourselves, Who am I to be brilliant, gorgeous, talented, and fabulous? Actually, who are you not to be? You are a child of God. Your playing small does not serve the world. There is nothing enlightened about shrinking so that other people will not feel insecure around you. We are all meant to shine, as children do. We were born to make manifest the glory of God that is within us. It is not just in some of us; it is in everyone and as we let our own light shine, we unconsciously give others permission to do the same. As we are liberated from our own fear, our presence automatically liberates others.'

Recipe for a Happy Child
Marina Cowdray

Love and more love.
Give your child a torch to hold, to lighten up the path of the walk called life.

Love and hug your child and feel in your heart a connection with your child's heart. Unconditional love will flourish.

Be the change you want to see in your child. Don't turn the child into you.

Trust your intuition: feelings are more powerful than responding to your mind.

There is no such thing as routine in nature. Nature expresses itself in every given moment, let the child be a natural expression of themselves.

Take responsibility wholeheartedly for yourself, and spend time in silence. Giving yourself peace of mind that in turn gives your child peace of mind.

See yourself as the child, and remember you were the child once. Play with the child and don't take on the burdens of the world. Your child is your world.

Resistance develops from being controlled. Parents are their own conditioning: your child will repeat patterns until you understand your true nature.

When you make a mistake, be able to look your child in the eye and say sorry, please forgive me.

Drop putting yourself in the parenting role, be patient and listen fully; there is no past, there is no future, there is only this moment.

Your child is not an expression of you, they are an expression of themselves.

Transparency breeds transparency, open conversations lead to open conversations. Indoctrination of any kind is a limitation, allow your child to find their own way.

Telephoning a child constantly doesn't make a good parent. Let the child go and let the child do the calling.

Substances fill a void; when there is no void, no substances are required. Any of your own addictions will be adopted by your child, so think carefully whether you want them to repeat your patterns.

If your child upsets you, recognise your own shortcomings. Love the difference between you and your child. Look at every challenge as a blessing.

Respect and trust in our children breeds success and trust in the world.

Encouragement breeds confidence.

Drop the false belief that fitting in and being top of the class and winning a game are the priorities; this moment is the priority and let that be good enough.

Home is a place of refuge; let the child have the space they need to be quiet.

Make homework fun, otherwise don't do it.

Have deep gratitude for your child and forgive them as they are trapped in your own conditioning.

Being the perfect parent is being who you truly are. Your child is your teacher, be open to learn from your child.

Your child will bring you more joy and love than you ever imagined.

The definition of courage
President Kennedy

Grace under pressure.

Truth, Joy, Kindness and Courage conquer all.

Endless thanks

Enormous thanks first of all to my editor, Sam Carter. Sam edited my last book, *10 Minute Suppers for Children*, and has worked his magic again here. It would not be the special book it is today without his influence and hard work. Thank you again to Ned Cranborne for introducing me to Sam four years ago.

To Charlotte Hepburn Scott who drew the stars on the cover of the book. I knew exactly which kind of stars I wanted to use, and Charlotte brought them to life so beautifully.

To my family: my mother, brother, sister and sister-in-law for their constant support and love.

To my friends who have contributed to this book by sending in their favourite poems, thank you so very much. It has been such a pleasure working on this project through the winter, and reading your favourites. My apologies to those whose poems are not here; there were stringent copyright laws which prohibited me publishing some beautiful poems.

To my meditation teacher, Burgs, and all at The Art of Meditation (theartofmeditation.org) who have profoundly influenced my life in the last few years.

To my godchildren: Otis, Ned, Louis, Laurie, Johnny,

Juno, Alice, Billy, Leila, Wren, Toto, Ivo, Evie and Mabel. I so hope you enjoy this book and it comes with love to you all.

To my own children, who assured me the book wouldn't sell, and that I shouldn't get my hopes up. I do so hope, on this one occasion, that you aren't right. This book is for you: Lorcan, Bertie, Pom and Jacobi, with all my love.

To Sean, thank you for everything.

Index of Poets

William Allingham 69
Saint Francis of Assisi 107

Hilaire Belloc 8, 13
William Blake 3, 4, 41
Emily Brontë 79
Rupert Brooke 40
Robert Burns 30

T. P. Cameron Wilson 1
Lewis Carroll 15, 22, 45, 58
C. P. Cavafy 94
G. K. Chesterton 11
Marina Cowdray 119
Elizabeth Craven 78

Dante 31, 34
John Dryden 91

Elizabeth I 98, 100
Ralph Waldo Emerson 6, 24

Rachel Field 7
Rose Fyleman 60

Adam Lindsay Gordon 90

Thich Nhat Hanh 114
William Randolph Hearst 80
W. E. Henley 37
Heinrich Hoffmann 92
Laurence Hope 23, 88
Bertie Hughes 57
Victor Hugo 33

R. G. Ingersoll 32

President Kennedy 122
Hazrat Inayat Khan 113
Rudyard Kipling 12, 67, 85

Emma Lazarus 89
Edward Lear 9, 51

A. A. Milne 62
John Milton 55, 82

Lady Nairne 26

Edgar Allan Poe 20

Christina Rossetti 28, 46, 56
Rumi 25

Siegfried Sassoon 17
Sir Walter Scott 39

William Shakespeare 87, 97
Percy Bysshe Shelley 48
Sir Philip Sidney 19
Christopher Smart 5
Cecil Spring-Rice 38
Robert Louis Stevenson 77

Alfred, Lord Tennyson 73
Ba'al Shem Tov 29

Mary Vivian 72

Charles Wesley 105
Marianne Williamson 118

William Butler Yeats 27, 74

The Essential Recipe Book for the Busy Parent…

10 Minute Suppers for children

by poppy fraser

www.poppyfraser.co.uk